LIVEWIRE
REAL LIVES

Sarah Michelle
Gellar

Julia Holt

Published in association with The Basic Skills Agency

Hodder & Stoughton
A MEMBER OF THE HODDER HEADLINE GROUP

Acknowledgements

Cover: © Peter Brooker/Rex Features.

Photos: p. 2 © 20th Century Fox/Rex Features; p. 7 © Paul Meaves/All Action Pictures Ltd; p. 12 © Walter McBride/Retna Ltd; p. 16 © SIPA/Rex Features; p. 21, 25 © BFI Stills, Posters and Designs; p. 26 © Araldo Di Crollalanza/Rex Features

Orders; please contact Bookpoint Ltd, 130 Milton Park, Abingdon, Oxon OX14 4SB. Telephone (44) 01235 827720, Fax: (44) 01235 400454. Lines are open from 9.00–6.00, Monday to Saturday, with a 24 hour message answering service. You can also order through our website www.hodderheadline.co.uk

British Library Cataloguing in Publication Data
A catalogue record for this title is available from the British Library

ISBN 0 340 87646 8

First published 2003
Impression number   10 9 8 7 6 5 4 3 2 1
Year   2009 2008 2007 2206 2005 2004 2003

Typeset by SX Composing DTP, Rayleigh, Essex.
Printed in Great Britain for Hodder & Stoughton Educational, a division of Hodder Headline, 338 Euston Road, London NW1 3BH by Bath Press Ltd, Bath.

Contents

1 The Chosen One

There will always be a chosen one.
She alone will stand against the vampires.
She will defy the demons.
She will stand against the forces of darkness.
She is the slayer.

Buffy Summers is the slayer.
She has been slaying
vampires and demons since 1997.
She is in the TV show
Buffy the Vampire Slayer.

Sarah Michelle Gellar as Buffy, the Vampire Slayer.

2 Sarah's Early Years

Sarah Michelle Gellar
plays the part of Buffy.
The show has made her a star.
She has fans all round the world.
This is just
what Sarah has always wanted.

Sarah was born in New York
on 14 April 1977.
Her parents split up
when she was little.
She stayed with her mum.

As a little girl
Sarah was always dreaming.
She wished she was on TV
or in a film.
Then one day, she was eating out
with her family.
She was spotted by an agent.

The agent asked Sarah
if she wanted to try acting.
The four year old said, 'Yes'.
From that day on, she has worked
in TV and films.

Some of the little girl's wages
paid for her to go to private schools.
But she didn't like school.
The other kids picked on her.
She was already working and they weren't.

Sometimes she had to choose.
Children's parties or acting.
She always chose acting.

Sarah's friends were not from school.
They were actors too.
When she was little
her best friend was Melissa.
She played *Sabrina, the Teenage Witch*.

When Sarah was five years old
she was in a Burger King advert.
She had to say
McDonald's burgers were too small.
McDonald's sued Sarah.
She became famous in the USA.
She went on to make 35 more adverts
for Burger King.

Sarah joined the actors' union.
But they don't allow two actors
to join with the same name.
There was already one Sarah Gellar.
So she used her middle name as well.
For acting work she used the name
Sarah Michelle Gellar.

Sarah, aged 5, on the TV show *Before They Were Famous*.

3 A Girl of Many Talents

Sarah's mum did not push her
to be an actor.
She made sure that she
did other things as well.

Sarah was a top ice dancer.
She did Tae Kwon Do.
Soon she was
at the top of that sport too.

The rest of the time
Sarah studied.
She studied her school work.
She studied TV shows.
Her mind was made up.
She wanted to be in a TV show.

In 1992, Sarah's life changed in three ways.

Her mum married again.

Sarah got her first part
in a TV soap.

It only lasted for a year
but it boosted her career.

Sarah found a school
that she liked.

It was a school for working children.

Some were dancers.

Some were actors.

But they were all gifted.

4 Her Big Break

At sixteen, Sarah
got a really big break.
She was given a part
in a TV soap in the USA.
It was called *All My Children*.

She played the long lost child
of the star of the show.
In the story she was nasty and spiteful.
Sarah was a smash hit.

She won an award for great acting.

Sarah left the show.
She left school
and she moved to California.
She looked for more work.

Sarah when she was in *All My Children*, at the Emmy
Awards in 1994.

5 Buffy is Mine

Back in 1992,
a man called Joss made a comedy film.
It was called *Buffy The Vampire Slayer*.
It was a big flop.
Joss said he would do it again as a TV horror show.

But who was going to play Buffy?

Sarah Michelle Gellar
knew the answer.
<u>She</u> wanted to play Buffy.
The people making the show said no.
They wanted her to play Cordelia.

So Sarah had to beg.
She made them think again.
She wanted the part of Buffy.
Very badly.
Sarah felt that Buffy was like her.
She also liked the story lines.
She got her own way.
The part of Buffy was hers.

6 *Buffy*: The Success Story

The show tells the story of Buffy Summers.
She lives in Sunnydale, California.
Sunnydale is a town
built over the 'Hellmouth'.
It is the door to hell.

Buffy is the only girl in the world
who can fight the vampires and demons.
She has family and friends
who help her.

The cast of *Buffy the Vampire Slayer*, 1999.

Buffy was first shown
in the USA in 1997.
The critics loved the show.
At first the public didn't watch it.
But by the end of the first series
it was a big hit.
The fans made websites.
They were about Buffy and her vampire
boyfriend, Angel.

Today, there are *Buffy* dolls, T-shirts and games.
A cartoon series is on its way.

All the team who work on *Buffy*
are proud of the show.
In each series there is something new.
There is a new kind of demon.
A new boyfriend.
A new problem.

Buffy grows older in the show as well.
In the first TV series she is a schoolgirl.
In the sixth series her mum has died.
Buffy looks after her little sister.
In other TV series, the actors never get any older.

7 Lights, Camera, Action!

Buffy has made Sarah
rich and famous.
She says it is what she has always wanted.
She moved into her first house.
It was in the Hollywood Hills.
She lived there with her two dogs.
Thor and Tyson.
Her mum lived close by in LA.

Every year, the *Buffy* team
has a three month break.
Sarah uses this time to make films.
In 1997, she made two.
They were both horror films.

The first was
I Know What You Did Last Summer.
It tells the story of four friends.
They go out driving one night.
They hit and kill a man.
Then they throw his body in the water.
They think no one will know.
Then someone starts to stalk them.

Sarah in *I Know What You Did Last Summer.*

Sarah and the other three actors
in the film
became close friends.
But one of them,
Freddie Prinze Jnr.,
became very special indeed.
In 2000, he became Sarah's boyfriend.

When the film came out
it topped the box office charts.
For two weeks.

Next Sarah had a small part
in *Scream 2*.
She gets killed early in the film.
Just in time to get back
to making the next series of *Buffy*.

8 Just Married!

In April 2001,
Sarah and Freddie got engaged.
Later that year
they moved into a $3 million villa in LA.
Sarah had always said
that she would not marry an actor.
But now she is with Freddie.

In the same year
Sarah jumped at the chance
to act with Freddie again.
This time it was for six months
in Australia.
They made the film *Scooby-Doo*.

Sarah as her character in *Scooby Doo*.

Sarah and Freddie
were married on 1 September 2002.
It was on the beach in Mexico.
Both of them wore white.
Sarah wore flip-flops.
There were 60 people
at the wedding.
All their family and friends.

Sarah had her three best friends
as bridesmaids.
The couple gave each other
platinum rings.
They had a short break.
Then they went back to work in LA.

Sarah and Freddie Prinze Jnr. at the premier of *Scooby-Doo*.

9 The Future

Sarah has been an actor
for over 20 years.
So what is there left for her to do?

She wants to write books
for children.
Or maybe open a café with Freddie.

People try to guess
how many series of *Buffy*
there will be.
And will there be
a new *Buffy* film?

What do you think?